NBA
by the numbers

by Bruce Brooks

with photographs from the
National Basketball Association

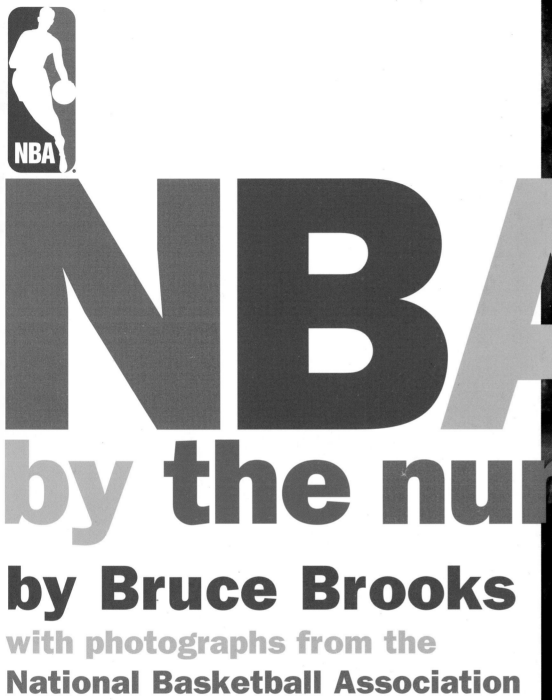

Scholastic Press
New York

Cover and book design by Charles Kreloff

Library of Congress Cataloging-in-Publication Data
NBA by the numbers by Bruce Brooks, with photos
from the NBA.   p.cm.
Summary: Photographs of notable basketball players
and text about the game are organized to represent
the numbers from one to fifty.
ISBN 0-590-97578-1
1. Basketball players—United States—Juvenile
literature. 2. National Basketball Association—
Juvenile literature. [1. Basketball. 2. Basketball
players. 3. Counting.] I. Title.
GV885.5.B76   1997
796.323 — dc2096-27327
CIP   AC

12 11 10 9 8 7 6 5 4 3 2 1   7 8 9/9 0 1 2/0
Printed in the U.S.A.   37
First printing, February 1997

Photo credits

Front cover: (clockwise from left) Andrew D. Bernstein, Andy Hayt, Nathaniel S. Butler.
Back cover: (top row left to right) Noren Trotman, Fernando Medina;
(middle row left to right) NBA Photo Library, Noren Trotman;
(bottom row left to right) Andrew D. Bernstein, Andrew D. Bernstein, Noren Trotman.
Page 1: Andrew D. Bernstein.
Page 5: Barry Gossage.
Page 6: NBA Photo Library.
Page 7: Richard Lewis.
Page 8-9: (left to right) Andrew D. Bernstein, NBA Photo Library, Nathaniel S. Butler.
Page 10-11: (clockwise from left) Chris Covatta, Jerry Wachter, Nathaniel S. Butler,
Ray Amati.
Page 12-13: (clockwise from left) Andrew D. Bernstein, Scott Cunningham,
Lou Capozzola, Scott Cunningham, Barry Gossage.
Page 14-15: (clockwise from left) Barry Gossage, Fernando Medina, Andy Hayt,
Nathaniel S. Butler, Barry Gossage, Lou Capozzola.
Page 16-17: (clockwise from left) Gregg Forwerck, Richard Lewis, Jeff Reinking,
Dale Tait, Rocky Widner, Dale Tait, Frank McGrath.
Page 18-19: (clockwise from left) Andrew D. Bernstein, Steve Woltmann, Tim Defrisco,
Al Messerschmidt, Andrew D. Bernstein, Noren Trotman, Andrew D. Bernstein,
Jon Soohoo.
Page 20-21: (clockwise from left) Andy Hayt, NBA Photo Library, Scott Cunningham,
Nathaniel S. Butler, Scott Cunningham, Jim Cummins, Jerry Wachter, Barry Gossage,
Jeff Reinking.
Page 22-23: Scott Cunningham.
Page 24-25: (Top row left to right) Noren Trotman, Fernando Medina,
Andrew D. Bernstein; (Middle row left to right) NBA Photo Library, Andy Hayt,
Noren Trotman, Andy Hayt; (Bottom row left to right) Andrew D. Bernstein,
Andrew D. Bernstein, Andy Hayt, Noren Trotman, Scott Cunningham, D. Clarke Evans.
Page 26-27: (clockwise from left to right) Fernando Medina, Noren Trotman, Steve
DiPaola, Gregg Forwerck, Fernando Medina, Noren Trotman, NBA Photo Library,
Chris Covatta, Noren Trotman, Chris Covatta.
Page 28-29: Dale Tait.
Page 30-31: All photos courtesy NBA Photo Library except the following:
(Top row) Abdul-Jabbar/Andrew D. Bernstein; Barkley/Vincent Manniello; Baylor/George
Kalinsky; Bird/Andrew D. Bernstein; (Second row) Drexler/Ron Hoskins; Ewing/Noren
Trotman; Gervin/Kevin Reece; (Third row) Johnson/Andrew D. Bernstein; Jordan/Scott
Cunningham; K. Malone/Scott Cunningham; McHale/Lou Capozzola; (Fourth row)
Olajuwon/Layne Murdoch; O'Neal/Andrew D. Bernstein; Parish/Andrew D. Bernstein;
Pippen/Scott Cunningham; Robinson/Chris Covatta; (Fifth row) Stockton/Layne
Murdoch; Thomas/Allen Einstein; Walton/Dick Raphael; Worthy/Nathaniel S. Butler.

NBA
by the numbers

1
Alert Dribbler

For a basketball player, dribbling should become as natural as walking. The guards in the NBA never need to look at the ball to make sure it's under control. They have spent so much time dribbling — left and right — since childhood, that they FEEL the ball as it falls to the floor, bounces and comes back up, as if it were a part of their hands.

2
Tricky Passers

A pass is simply the fastest way to get the ball to an open teammate. Some great passes are sneaky and deceptive — flipping the ball behind your back to the left while you are driving to the right, or heading straight at the defender, looking him in the eyes, then whipping the ball blind to a teammate. Some great passes are plain and obvious — they cannot be stopped no matter how clearly a defender can see them coming — they just get the job done.

3
Smart Layups

If a team could free one player for a layup every time down the floor, it would gladly take nothing but layups all season (and probably wouldn't lose a single game). Shooting from close in is usually worth the trouble it takes to get there with the ball. It's generally more efficient than shooting from farther away from the hoop, whether the layup is easy — when you freeze three defenders flat-footed in the paint and float up yourself to drop it through; or difficult — when you are so well-guarded that you have to loft the ball back over your head high off the glass, or when you must work the ball through a quick gap OVER one defender's arm and UNDER another's.

4
Determined Shotblockers

An NBA player learns never to give up. Even when a shooter DOES get a chance to lay the ball up from close in, a defender won't want to make it easy for him. One final weapon remains to be used, one final challenge: The defender can block the shot, smothering the ball in the shooter's hand or swatting it out of the air just after the shooter releases. Shotblocking is not just a matter of height, and not everyone can do it. It takes good timing, quick hands, and an aggressive attitude: "Nothing gets by ME easy."

5
Focused Defenders

Great defense requires great concentration. You can try to anticipate what your man will do, but mostly you have to be ready to react when he DOES do something — react so fast that you match him step for step and leap for leap, always staying between him and the hoop. Four of these defenders have been both quick and patient, holding perfect position, so that the would-be shooter has no options and will either hold the ball too long or make a desperate pass. But one of these defenders has been too eager: He anticipated a little TOO much and left his feet before the man with the ball did.

6
Snatching Rebounders

Every team tries to play defense so that the opponent can only take hard shots that won't go in. When a shot misses, the ball is up for grabs. Great rebounders grab it. They turn from playing D and keep their man away from the ball with their back and hips; or, if they are on the shooting team, they try to sneak by their man and slice to the basket for a quick snatch or a surprise tip. Sometimes a rebound causes a grand battle between three or four or six players, all trying to time their leaps so they get that extra inch of reach that gives them control.

7
Clutch Free Throw Shooters

Sometimes the only way a defender can stop a great offensive player is to foul him. Though the move is stopped, the ballhandler or shooter gets his fair chance to score anyway. He steps to the free throw line, 15 feet away from the backboard, with everyone watching, the ball in his hands to dribble, squeeze, and spin. Will he deliver in the clutch? The frenzied fans wait for him to take his shot: a cool-headed, no-doubt swish, or an unnerved brick off the back iron. Good players practice a lot, concentrate, and stay cool in the clutch.

8
Loose Balls

Chaos! The ball is bouncing free. When this happens, any scrappy player's instinct kicks in automatically: "GET IT!" In the NBA every possession is precious, every loose ball worth fighting for. Sometimes, though, that round thing is pretty difficult to hang on to....

9
Slammin' Dunkers

The best way to make absolutely sure the ball goes in the hoop, of course, is to jam it. In the old days only the big guys would dunk regularly. But in today's NBA, everyone's always ready to make that electrifying leap.

10
Elite Players

The fact is, every player in the NBA is a basketball star. Every player, even the one who waits at the end of the bench to step in for six minutes and help his team somehow, was probably the best guy by far on every other team he ever played on, from junior high school on. In their past play, most of these stars have been able to rely on having superior talent over everyone else on the floor. But not anymore. Now every man you face is supremely talented (and quick, and crafty, and determined). If talent is everywhere, the only way you can rise above the other guys is to work harder, concentrate longer, hustle more. It's pretty competitive out there.

20
Sensational Shoes

We all watch the hands of the players most of the time, because that's where the ball moves. But the fundamental game of basketball is played down lower, right on the floor, with the feet. It's the feet that cut and stop, the feet that hold defensive position, the feet that square up to the hoop before launching the man high for a good-look jump shot. Sneaker technology (and style) has come a long way in the past few years, but remember — it's not the shoes that make the moves. It's the feet inside. Pay attention to them. They'll take you as far as you want to go.

30
Downtown Points

The three-point shot added a new dimension of excitement to NBA basketball. An offense can now be built around TWO excellent options: get the ball close to the hoop for a layup or kick it out to your hawkeye for the long ball. And, hey, making a 22-foot jump shot is HARD. The man who can hit it deserves the extra point.

40
Frantic Fingers

When it comes down to it, basketball could be called a game of fingertips. They're the first things to touch the ball when you take possession; they're the last things to let it go when you shoot or pass. The great Dr. J (Hall of Famer Julius Erving), was often asked what the secret of his astonishing play was, and he often disappointed his audience with the plainness of his answer: "I was born with extremely long fingers, and sensitive fingertips. They let me hold the ball a little longer, wait until I saw my opening, and then shoot with a little more control than most guys. You'd be surprised what a difference a finger makes."

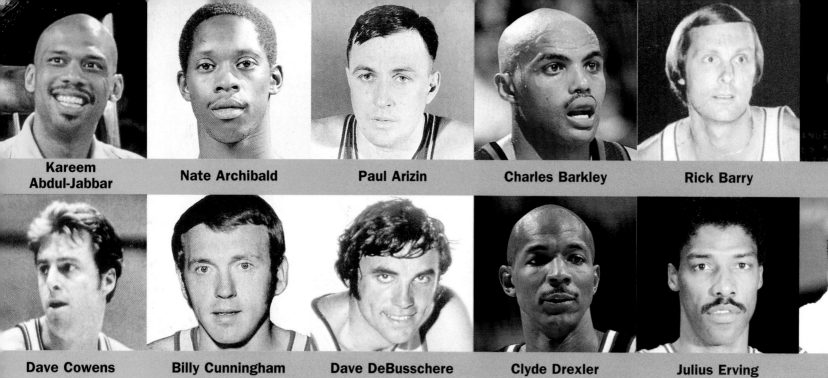

| Kareem Abdul-Jabbar | Nate Archibald | Paul Arizin | Charles Barkley | Rick Barry | Elgin Bayl|

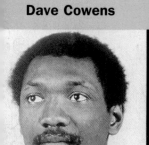   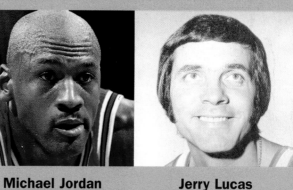 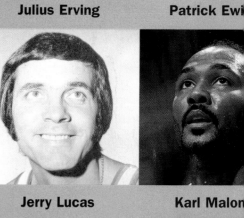

| Dave Cowens | Billy Cunningham | Dave DeBusschere | Clyde Drexler | Julius Erving | Patrick Ewi|

  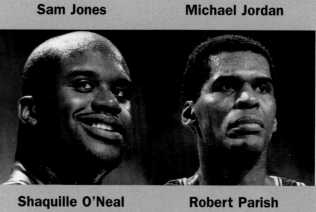 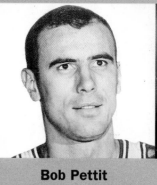

| Elvin Hayes | Earvin Johnson | Sam Jones | Michael Jordan | Jerry Lucas | Karl Malon|

| Earl Monroe | Hakeem Olajuwon | Shaquille O'Neal | Robert Parish | Bob Pettit | Scottie Pipp|

| Dolph Schayes | Bill Sharman | John Stockton | Isiah Thomas | Nate Thurmond | Wes Unsel|

Dave Bing

Larry Bird

Wilt Chamberlain

Bob Cousy

50
All-Time
Stars

Walt Frazier

George Gervin

Hal Greer

John Havlicek

Moses Malone

Pete Maravich

Kevin McHale

George Mikan

To celebrate its 50th anniversary, the NBA has chosen these players as the 50 greatest of all time. In here are shooters, stealers, rebounders, passers, thinkers, leaders — not every player could do everything perfectly in this demanding game, but each had something extraordinary to give to his team and the game. What new players will be here among the finest of the fine in another 50 years? One thing is certain: The best will find their way to the courts of the NBA and will have the chance to show what they can do. The game is always ready for the players.

Willis Reed

Oscar Robertson

David Robinson

Bill Russell

Walton

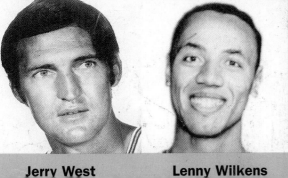

Jerry West

Lenny Wilkens

James Worthy

Index of Key Players
(All photos are listed clockwise from left except where noted)